HO

MAGIC MONEY MASTERY

A COURSE IN
CREATING
ABUNDANCE

BOOK THREE

HOLLY ALEXANDER

MAGIC MONEY

MASTERY

A COURSE IN CREATING ABUNDANCE

BOOK THREE

Published by Magic Money Books

Copyright 2017 © Magic Money Books

All rights reserved. No part of this book may be reproduced or transmitted in any form or by any means, electronic or mechanical, including photocopying, recording or by any information storage and retrieval system without written permission of the publisher, except for the inclusion of brief quotations in a review.

Paperback ISBN: 978-1-947665-01-9

Digital ISBN: 978-1-947665-00-2

YOU'RE INVITED

I would like to personally invite you to the Magic Money Books community at Facebook.com/groups/MagicMoneyBooks where you can join in on the magic! You'll find daily support, affirmations, and inspiration from like-minded individuals on their own magic money journey.

I'd also love to hear from you personally! You can connect with me through email at Holly@MagicMoneyBooks.com. I look forward to connecting and hearing about your magic money journey soon!

TABLE OF CONTENTS

Chapter One:
Magic Money Mastery 1

Chapter Two:
Preparing for Your Third
Magic Money Experiment:
Mastery Living 7

Chapter Three:
Engaging the Magic Every Day 13

Chapter Four:
The Seven Magic Money Steps
for Life 25

Chapter Five:
Days-of-the-week Fun with
Magic Money 35

Chapter Six:
Prosperity Practices for
More Magic Money 47

Chapter Seven:
Magic Everything 63

Chapter Eight:
A Lifetime of Magic Money:
Your Final Magic Money Experiment 77

Gratitude 81

Who is Holly 83

Dear Reader,

Welcome to *Magic Money Mastery*, the third and final installment in a three-book series. If you've stumbled upon this book before reading *Beginning Magic Money* and *Advanced Magic Money*, you'll want to start at the beginning and eventually find yourself back here.

This part of the Course is designed to solidify what you've learned so far. Embracing the Magic Money Philosophy will allow you to create complete and total financial independence, enrich your life in every way, and allow you to live a life of magic, miracles, and abundance in an easy way…*for life*.

My intention for you is to finally shed any limiting money beliefs that remain and adopt a new truth: you inhabit a generous Universe, and it wants to give you the best of everything. Liberally and effortlessly. I want you to know beyond a shadow of a doubt you are cared for, provided for, and all is well *all the time*.

The first two books in the course have brought you to here, right now. When you're ready, turn the page.

Your magical life awaits!

Holly Alexander

Chapter One

MAGIC MONEY MASTERY

Magic Money is the wonderful abundance (including money) you attract into your life in expected and unexpected ways through the practice of the Magic Money Philosophy.

As you now know, the Magic Money Philosophy can be summed up in these twenty-seven words:

Focus the endless energy of your mind on abundance, and treat all you receive with respect, and you will have unlimited abundance—because of, or despite, what is happening around you.

By the time you read this book, you will have experienced some mind-blowing experiences with money. And, you will know Magic Money isn't just about money because you've had some other magical things happen. Right? Right!

Perhaps you've received money out of the blue, like Experimenter Kyle:

So today I got an email, out of the blue. A tech company I used to work for was reaching out to verify my contact and banking information so they could send me a residual stock payment. I left that job four years ago. That, my friends, is magic money.

Or, like Teresa, received the exact amount you need just in the nick of time:

After buying groceries, this past weekend I emptied our checking account until my husband's paycheck comes in this Friday, I was trying to figure out how I was going to pay for the haircuts I had scheduled for my two kids and myself tomorrow. I had agreed last month to watch a friend's 6-year-old daughter today, and when picking her up a little while ago, my friend handed me some cash for my time. When I saw how much it was, and combined it to the money already in my wallet, I realized it was EXACTLY how much I needed (to the dollar). #holymagicmoney

Or, like Brenda, you'll receive a surprise that can only be described as Magic Money-in-action:

I got behind schedule yesterday because I received a big ole letter from the bank. Turns out, for a mere $140 we could pay off the house. SO I ran down there to get 'er done! Wow, eh? I knew we were paying a little extra each month, but to pay it off over ten years early was a surprise. How's that for magic money!? It rocks!

You have a long list of manifestations, and you're ready to step fully into the flow of an abundance of all things, including money. Am I right?

I thought so, which is why I'm writing this book (and I almost didn't). It took me *years* to fully step into the place where I could trust I would always have more than enough no matter what. To commit to the Magic Money Philosophy and allocate all funds in the way I described in *Advanced Magic Money* (even when my liquidity looked to be at an all-time low, and I *might* have to dip into long-term capital). It took a few times of going from abundant to frantic to rich, well and happy back to frustrated and finally back to wealthy for me to *g-e-t i-t*. Ahem, yup, that's right—I'm *human.*

After sharing *Beginning Magic Money* with a few dozen wonderful humans and seeing their delightful (and shocked) reactions, I knew I needed to go ahead and write this book.

Because I'm human, and I care about people, it has been hard for me to watch others struggle. All the time knowing a few fundamental shifts, along with some practical actions, could make all the difference. I no longer wanted anyone I could touch to strain and strive when they could "Magic Money" and thrive!

And, in addition to the daily or weekly Magic Money practices I've described, there are simple actions I take on a regular basis to keep the flow coming. Upon reflection, I knew without insight and these extra little goodies, you might only use Magic Money for a finite amount of time. It occurred to me that it was entirely possible Magic Money might be something you practiced for a time and then forgot to keep using. Without turning the Magic Money Philosophy into your way of life, it would remain something you *do,* instead of becoming who you *are.*

That realization made me clear the decks and begin writing. It just didn't sit right with me that anyone would discover almost enough to live an abundant life—but not have *the rest of the story* (as Paul Harvey was famous for saying). It wasn't enough for me to share the recipe for the most delicious cake you've ever tasted, and then neglect to give you the recipe for the icing as well. And help you set up auto-replenishment!

So, here we are, and I can hardly contain my excitement as I begin to share with you everything you need to live the rest of your life as an abundant human being. With insight into practices, along the way I've uncovered to receive money every day in expected and unexpected ways. To give and receive with grace and ease. To smile and look up when yet another incredible windfall shows up, or I meet just the right person at the right time, or I get a new client at the perfect time in the perfect way.

You might know by now I'm the most practical and pragmatic person to walk the earth (really). And if you knew me personally, you wouldn't believe this no-nonsense, professional person was tithing, saying affirmations, updating her vision board, and making a daily list of desired manifestations. And then sitting back and letting the Universe do most of the heavy lifting.

You would probably think, as 99.98% of the people in my life do, that I work twenty hours a day with the focus and determination of a lioness on the hunt for food for her young.

And, I don't. I practice every single action in *Beginning Magic Money* and *Advanced Magic Money*, as well as what I share in this book.

But this is not about me; you're here because you want *more*. You want to struggle less and prosper more. You want less stress and more happiness. You want more of what you've experienced over the past month or two, and less of what you've been struggling with for perhaps your entire life.

It's time, and I can hardly wait.

Chapter Two

PREPARING FOR YOUR SECOND MAGIC MONEY EXPERIMENT:

Mastery Living

As I shared in *Advanced Magic Money*, the creator of the rich universe we live in *can* provide an abundance of everything we could ever possibly want or use. First, we must identify our desires and allow them to come into our lives through our thoughts, words, and actions.

Then we must commit fully to the practices that allow them to appear.

YOUR SECOND MAGIC MONEY EXPERIMENT

I think I did a pretty darn good job of making it sound simple right there, didn't I? If it were that easy, then everyone would be doing it, right?

Well, it is and they could be. *You could be.*

In fact, I know if you're reading this you have already experienced some "easy money" from reading the first two books and doing your first two experiments. You're thinking, *Yup, I'll be wanting some more of THAT!*

And you can have it, all of it you want. Your third, and final Magic Money Experiment isn't for a week or a month or even a year. It is *for life*.

You won't allocate *some* of your income as I've outlined in *Advanced Magic Money*, you'll allocate *all* of it! You won't think, say, and do the practices that work *sometimes*—you'll do them **all the time** (and the more you do them, the better you'll get). Also, you'll add the practices I share in this book if they resonate with you.

Pull out your Magic Money Journal, light a candle, make a cup of tea (or pour yourself a glass of something delightful), and get ready. It's time for *Magic Money Mastery*.

Setting Your Life-Long Intention

Setting an intention sounds (and is) so easy you might squint your eyes and think, *This can't be it. It's too easy.* And, my abundant friend, you would be wrong. It is just this easy.

In one simple sentence, decide just how abundantly you want to live the rest of your life. You might want just enough to live comfortably and without stress, or you might want to become the world's 1,811th billionaire. Up to you, my friend. If you can think it, then to become it, you must ink it.

Here's my Magic Money Intention:

I always have more than enough to give, save, share, and spare, and my needs and desires are always met (on time or early).

Although it has gone through a few iterations, I crafted the first version of that sentence almost thirty years ago. Since then, I have always had *enough*. I've received *every single thing* I've ever truly wanted—sometimes long before I needed it, and sometimes with (literally!) seconds to spare. The longer I practiced the Magic Money Philosophy, the better I got at it. The more I trusted the process, ignored my fear and focused

YOUR SECOND MAGIC MONEY EXPERIMENT

on my desired outcome, the easier life became. Not just about money, about everything!

Here are just a few examples:

- I bought a fully-furnished home. With cash. A year after I walked into it and declared, *This is my home.*

- Within forty-eight hours, (and after being told it was impossible), I found the exact car I wanted. The buyer became a client and ultimately paid for it *four times over* in consulting fees.

- I met and married the exact man no-one thought existed—except me.

- With no advanced education, I have a career that allows me to charge thousands of dollars *per hour* for my time.

———

You might notice I didn't put a number on my intention. That wasn't the case at first. When I first started, I believed I had to have a certain dollar amount in reserve. This was based upon society's conditioning you "must have enough saved and invested for retirement."

I initially called this my (pardon my French) "fuck you number." The amount of money I wanted to have invested that generated more than enough monthly income to cover all of my expenses.

I created multiple streams of income, put away ten percent of every dollar, and eventually hit that number.

After about a decade, I realized it wasn't a number I needed to feel abundant. In fact, the more money I had, the more vulnerable I felt! Someone might sue me and take it. Or if I needed to tap into it, I would end up with a massive tax bill. The list went on, but you get the idea.

I realized what I wanted was a *feeling*. A sense of knowing all needs are met on time or early, and I could rest, relax, and recharge as necessary. For the rest of my life.

I didn't want to "retire" or quit working. In fact, I'm right at home while I'm working. I *love* to work because I love what I do (so it doesn't feel like work). But, as we all know too well, a hard work ethic doesn't always translate into abundance. There are a lot of hard working people in the world who struggle to make it from paycheck to paycheck.

Don't get me wrong, if you want to quantify your wealth with a number, do it! If you want to have a huge pile of money so you can stop working, more power to you! Whatever works best for you is what works best for you. *And you can have it.*

The longer you practice the Magic Money Philosophy, the better you'll get at it. The more you'll trust the process. The more opportunities you'll have to see it work. Your list of manifestations will grow and become irrefutable evidence you don't need to stress about money (or anything else)!

Grab your Journal and write the first draft of your life's Magic Money Intention. You will probably find over time, as I did, you'll want to change/update it until it feels just right.

Then, continue reading. The magic is about to get more magical.

Chapter Three

ENGAGING THE MAGIC EVERY DAY

You might notice, as the Experimenters did, some days are more magical than others. Some days, you'll feel like you're on a roll and money is coming from everywhere. Other days, you might not feel very magical or see any magic money.

After decades of practice, I find, receive, or earn money every single day. Yesterday I received an unexpected dividend, this morning it was a bonus check from a business I haven't been involved in for over a decade.

Your role in the magic is to think, say, and do "the magic money." The Universe will take care of the rest.

Oh, but you're either thinking *That's too easy*, or *That will never work*. Or both.

Stay with me here.

There will be days when you need money like you need air. Other days, you'll check your bank balance(s) and see you've got "enough." Eventually, you will reach the stage of being unattached because you have a deep, cellular knowing you are taken care of at all times, in all ways, no matter what. *All is well.*

This final, life-long magic money stage is fun and relaxing because you no longer need to check your balance or balance your checkbook (that's a job for your bookkeeper or accountant).

One of the reasons I started you off with just a few steps is because there are so many wonderful ways to engage the magic. It is easy to get overwhelmed or to try to jump levels without turning the fundamentals from actions to habits to *who you are*.

I'm unmoved by a lower bank balance, fewer sales or clients, or taking downtime. I know there are cycles of massive abundance, followed by periods of spending, vacationing, investing in new ventures, and splurging on a shiny new object. As I do all Seven Daily Magic Money Steps, all is well. And all remains well.

Daily Magic

Before I review the Seven Daily Magic Money Steps, it is important for me to share with you a couple of nuances to the Magic Money Philosophy. These are great to have in mind as you work your way into pure Magic Money Mastery.

You will receive plenty of Magic Money in the form of actual money (such as expected and unexpected income). You'll also receive free goods, discounted or free services, new clients, better-paying customers, and incredible opportunities.

Hopefully, you will add the Magic Money Philosophy to your way of being forever. You will enjoy an ever-increasing level of abundance if you engage the magic daily. However, even if you commit to a daily practice and you never let

ENGAGING THE MAGIC EVERY DAY

up on your accelerator, there will be delays and denials on your journey.

Not a day goes by I don't experience *something cool*. Even if I stay in pajamas and on my couch—I still have a magical conversation, text exchange, get a notice of a direct deposit, receive an email inquiry from a potential client, sell some extra products, or get a note from a friend.

And, there are a few things I've had on my list for quite some time. I never give up, because I now understand the process. But! It took some hard knocks, deep thinking, and some realizations (I can be a slow learner, that doesn't help) to fully understand what I'm about to share with you.

So, before I review your Magic Money steps, and add in other actions you can take to keep the magic engaged in your life, you need to understand two things:

- *The longer you wait, the better the result.*
- *Rejection is protection.*

The Longer You Wait, the Better the Result!

Look at your first Master List. Has anything on it manifested for you yet? I bet there are at least a couple of things you've crossed off your list because they showed up right away—and several more you're still waiting to manifest.

I can't tell you the number of times I've put something on my Master List and no sooner has the ink dried, I've received my desired item or situation. Thousands of times in my professional career I've manifested clients or high-paying opportunities, sold more than my desired quota, or found myself in the right place at the right time. Yes, thousands. I've lost count (and so will you).

Hindsight is always twenty-twenty, and I can look back over the last thirty years of my life and see where I was steered in a definite direction. Some of those times I distinctly remember being face-planted in a pool of snot and tears—although it turns out I was led in a definite and positively fantastic direction.

Let me let you in on a little secret: the longer you must wait for something on your list, the better it turns out to be!

For example, I had my sights set on a certain position within one company, and no matter how hard I worked I just couldn't break through. A simple sixty-second conversation gave me an idea that has turned into millions of dollars of income (and I no longer have a job)!

For *years*, I had been courting a client. When he finally said yes, I was less than convinced. He signed the contract, and brought his new business partner in on our conversations. Six years later we all still work together and are great friends.

There are multiple dozens of other examples, but suffice it to say if you're still waiting for something, and you've followed the suggestions in *Beginning Magic Money* and *Advanced Magic Money*, the better it will be when it shows up.

Or…

Rejection is Protection

Alternatively, I've learned *rejection is protection*. Some things sound like such an amazing idea or goal, but no matter how much we visualize, intend, affirm, and put it on our lists, our efforts come up snake eyes.

I used to think I was not manifesting correctly. I just need to be more committed, do more affirmations, or have a clearer picture in my mind. If I just held the vision in my mind a little longer, had a better picture on my vision board, or were a better person *then* what I wanted would come to me.

But when you're an old timer like I am, you have many years to look back on. Without question, a review of your history can (and does!) provide insight. I believe the Universe has my back and it intervenes when it knows I could be getting myself into a big pickle.

I found what I was sure was *the house* I would buy and live in for at least two decades. I turned in my offer three hours too late and missed out. Or did I? That house lost 60% of its value when the market crashed in 2008—and the owners lost almost two million dollars. Instead, I bought my apartment-turned-condo and enjoyed a 350% return on investment within nine months.

I thought I wanted to be with "that guy." Turns out—not a good fit (and we'd need a bottle of wine and a few hours for that story). Hint: turns out he didn't prefer women (ahem) … Bonus: the guy I'm with is so much more awesome!

When you're getting a big fat goose egg, and you're doing *everything* "*right*," consider that rejection might just be protecting you from something you'll look back on later and think, *Man, I dodged a bullet!* Said another way, if you must try hard for something with little or no encouragement or results, it might not be for your highest and best good!

I see so many people (internet marketers, I'm looking right at you!) trying *so hard* to create the exact right approach, copy, image, etcetera and so on. What they are missing is that magic money, success, and abundance easily flows when they are in the right state to receive it.

When you allow the Universe-at-large to orchestrate your desired results, what you want ends up landing right in your lap! In an easy way. With some fun sprinkled on top for good measure.

In my consulting business, I have had easy clients and difficult clients. I've spent time trying to *do* the right things—the right marketing, putting the right information in my email newsletter, appearing on the right television and radio shows (remember my super-expensive publicist?), guest blogging, and so many other activities.

Even though I *knew* I just needed to vibrate at a high frequency, live with an attitude of gratitude, and *be* positively expectant, I was determined to do it the hard way.

I remember the exact day when I decided to analyze exactly how my best and most wonderful clients appeared in my life, and here is what I discovered:

- Every single one came through "kismet" or what some describe as destiny. They randomly found out about me through a random conversation or by doing a Google search (note: I am *not* search engine optimized by any stretch of the imagination).

- They showed up, ready to pay my full fee, with the enthusiasm of a six-year-old on Christmas morning.

- They took my advice and got great results.

- Bonus: our relationships still last until this day, and sometimes we even still work together!

Not one client or customer found me through a brochure, ad, or targeted marketing (not the great ones, anyway). Once I realized the magical combination was me at my best combined with the forces of the Universe, I decided I liked this easier way of being and decided to embrace it full time. (Thanks, Universe! You rock!)

You know what? It has worked like a charm!

Now I have a process people need to go through to get on my calendar. They must apply to be my clients and agree to pay lots of money for my time. *Cheerfully.* No cheer, no consult! Once I set those boundaries, the right and perfect clients started coming to me easily and effortlessly. I always have the exact amount of work (if we could call it work), and money, I need. *Always.*

If you think it can't be that easy, I promise you *it is!* When you treat yourself, the world, and your money with respect, *it truly is that easy.* Ask for what you want, do what you know works, then let the Universe handle *everything* while you binge watch some Netflix. If it's meant to be, it will be! Or, something even better will show up.

You decide what you want, do your part to engage the magic, and watch with awe at what happens next!

Now, let's briefly review the Seven Magic Money Steps *for Life*. Then, just in case you feel like you need to actually "do" something to keep the magic money flowing, I'll share additional Magic Money practices that work like a charm.

Chapter Four

THE SEVEN MAGIC MONEY STEPS
for Life

As I shared with you in *Beginning Magic Money*, the Magic Money Philosophy consists of seven specific steps. To fully engage in a life-long practice of Magic Money, you must go deeper with each of the steps.

Remember, Magic Money flows based upon just a few things you *do*, and most importantly, based on who you're *being*.

Now that you have experienced the flow of Magic Money into your life, I'm certain you want to keep it going. Why else would you still be reading, right?

The Seven Magic Money Steps

Here I review each step, take you a bit deeper into each one, and then give you my current practice.

Number One: *Take control of what you think, say, and do with money.*

Money is good because money supports everything you do. You must think about money as good, talk about money as though it is good, and treat money with more and more respect as time passes.

When you speak about money, I suggest you adopt a mantra you repeat many times daily. Here are some of my favorites:

- *Money is awesome!*
- *I love money and money loves me!*
- *I always have more than enough money.*

- *Money comes to me, in increasing amounts, every single day.*

I say this one every time I pay for something:

As money goes out, immediately double the money comes back to me!

Every time I buy something, pay a bill, order something online, or get coffee at Starbucks, I silently or out loud say to myself: *As money goes out, immediately double the money comes back to me! As I spend $5, I give thanks $10 is on its way to me now in God's own wise and wonderful way!*

My mantra doesn't have to be your mantra, not even close. But I promise you a regular mantra, said consistently, will seep into your subconscious mind. And remember when I said this silent but oh-so-powerful player in the prosperity game needs to be kept happy? This is one fool-proof way to do it!

Decide what you want your first mantra to be, commit it to memory and get in the habit of saying it many times every day.

Number Two: *Suspend disbelief.*

What is it you desire? Most likely just the ability to pay your bills with only a few bucks to spare isn't your exactly your heart's desire. You want something incredible, and it might seem out of your reach.

In fact, I would guess you have your eye on at least one shiny object. Perhaps, up until recently, you didn't think it was possible for you. I can also imagine there's someone in your life, either directly or a few degrees removed, you'd like to do something awesome for—someone putting themselves through school and shouldering debt and you'd like to pay it off? A friend or family member trying to finance a business and you'd like to be an angel investor? Or maybe you want a fully-loaded Bentley Continental GT and cannot imagine how on God's green Earth you of all people could not only afford one but could pay for oil changes, new tires, and other regular maintenance. Roger that. And guess what? *It is entirely possible.* **For you.**

Whatever it is, whenever you think about it, you immediately also think, *but that's not possible for me,* this's the thing you must begin to entertain the thought is indeed possible for you!

You don't have to know how it will happen. Or when. Or through what channel. But by now, haven't you had some money and other abundance show up? And you could not have predicted it would have happened in (approximately) one hundred and twenty million years. Right?

Note: If you can't think of anything off hand, go back and consult your Magic Money Journal. There's at least a couple of instances in there. It's totally fine; I'll wait.

Suspend any disbelief you have left your desire is not possible, and begin to wonder how the Universe is going to pull this one off!

Number Three: *Let go of every belief you have that money must come to you through specific channels (i.e., through your job/career, an individual or entity, etc.).*

This just might be my favorite one, because, as I was just discussing, above, our channels of abundance can come at any time and in literally zillions of ways.

Letting go of this belief is particularly helpful if you have a boss you don't particularly care for or a job that requires you to do something that might appear in a *Dirty Jobs* episode. Are you kissing the ass of your rich Aunt Jane, hoping when she dies she leaves you her fortune—but you can't stand her? You can believe me when I say you don't have to engage in horrifying activities or put up with someone. There isn't one singular way you'll get your stream of magic money. In fact, the longer you try to maneuver your way through the Universe, the more it's going to give you a big fat eye roll and withhold what you've got coming your way.

Make sense? Good!

Instead, open yourself up to the possibilities and allow money to come to you through any channel it pleases. You could even go crazy and expect it to come! Wonder out loud as you towel off from your morning shower just how some money is going to come to you that day. Check your mail and email with the expectation of an unexpected check or notification of a refund, direct deposit, referral fee, or—well, who knows! The Universe can conjure up some great ideas while you're getting your beauty sleep.

Number Four: *Think and speak about money in a positive way.*

You must, from this point forward, intentionally think positive thoughts and say positive words about money every time you think about or talk about it.

Money and evidence of money is everywhere. It was used to pave the roads you drive on, build the Starbucks you visit every morning, and hang the lines bringing you electricity. Take a moment or five every day to realize how much money and abundance you get to use at little or no charge. Express gratitude for the free pen you got at the bank, the free Wi-Fi, email, or even computer you get to use, and the donut you just ate your boss grabbed on the way into the office. There are so many ways to think and speak about money in a positive way—all you must do is keep your eyes open and express your gratitude for it to multiply repeatedly.

Number Five: *Allow money to come to you from anywhere at any time.*

Slightly different from Number Three, this is the state of *allowing* money to flow to you from wherever it feels like coming. Does it matter if you get a check from the company you work for, or someone leaves a big bag of money on your doorstep? I didn't think so, and I'm open to both of those possibilities (and an unlimited number of others) myself. I'm unconcerned about where the money comes from, and it's perfectly fine if I receive a huge deposit into my bank account while I'm sleeping. I'm suggesting you get okay with this, too! I, myself, am open to "doorstep money presents" and have a couple of stories I'll share in a later book.

Number Six: *Believe there's more than enough for you now and henceforth forever.*

Money really is like air! There is, and will always be, more than enough for you when you keep your mind and heart open and expectant. Haven't your needs always been met? Don't all the bills eventually get paid, and at some point, you get or have what you need? That isn't going to stop, in fact, the more you embrace the concept that there's more than enough, the more there shall be.

Number Seven: *An abundance of everything you need is indeed on its way to you right now.*

Take a deep breath and *know* today is the first day you have more than enough of what you need. From now until forever, every single one of your needs are met, your bills are paid, and *even cooler than that*, anything you decide you want is on its way to you the minute you decide you want it.

Isn't it time for you to be open to receive all you want out of life, including money and an abundance of anything and everything you want and need? I think so! No, I *know* so! Working through each of the above steps will ensure you have a steady stream of magic money and an abundance of everything else flowing to you unendingly.

When you can embrace, and execute the above seven steps, you will be fully in the flow state of receiving magic money. Would you like a few more easy ways to do just that? I thought you would.

Chapter Five
DAYS-OF-THE-WEEK FUN
with Magic Money

Please keep in mind you can simply do the Seven Magic Money Steps to keep your vibration high and your wallet smack dab in the middle of a continuous flow of abundance.

But, as I mentioned, sometimes we can't quite accept *magic money is that easy*, and we want to do something. And, the easiest way to keep the magic flowing is to stay consistent with your daily actions. Easier said than done, though, right? Not really!

If you must do something, I've learned *fun* is key to becoming a Magic Money Master. Staying in the practice of Magic Money Mastery requires a consistent refocusing of our minds until actions become habits, and then those habits become who you *are*. I made the connection between *fun* and *money* and I want you to do the same.

More fun equals more magic money.

The magic money fun in my house started with Feel Good Fridays. After a week of work (for my husband and me) and school (for our daughter), we would always gear up to do something fun on the weekends. Preparation included a trip to the grocery store where we stock up on all the snacks and drinks we could every possibly need. I realized I had enjoyed my weekends more because of what I was doing on Fridays. The more enjoyable my Fridays and weekends, the more magic money flowed into the life during the week that followed.

I nicknamed every Friday, "Feel Good Fridays" and soon every day of the week had a special name, too. I'm going to share my what I do each day of the week, and I encourage you to customize your days, too.

Why?

Because what you focus on expands, and it is easy to lose or change your focus. By identifying something definite to focus on each day, you will keep your positive energy high and your magic money flowing!

Feel Good Fridays

About ten years ago, I agreed to host a feng shui workshop in my home. The instructor "feng shui'd" my entire house in return. I've kept many of the practices, including always having fresh flowers in my home. Feng shui uses flowers as a symbol to evoke feelings of beauty, grace, and aliveness. I use them to brighten my personal space! Fresh flowers just *feel good*, and they are one of the fastest and easiest ways to shift and raise the energy and vibration of your environment.

I prefer live flowers, and my instructor said they are the premier choice for your home because they bring a strong healing energy (as opposed to silk or other fake flowers). Flowers bring with them the great energies of natural beauty and grace, as well as good luck, numerous blessings, and quality of Chi (also known as universal great energy). And, great energy is a catalyst for Magic Money!

I usually grab a mixed bunch of flowers that include sunflowers. I love sunflowers because they are bright and beautiful, and they make me feel happy. If you are home most of the time, you can also schedule a weekly flower delivery subscription service. Remember your work space, too—fresh flowers feel amazing at the office. When I'm traveling, I try to have fresh flowers in my hotel room. And, as soon as I get home, I get a new bouquet and put it in the most beautiful vase I can find.

Adding colorful, fresh flowers to your home immediately changes the energy to feel lighter, happier, and more vibrant. This energy is infectious and brightens your energy and mood (and that of anyone you live with, too!). When choosing your flowers, pick the ones you are the most attracted to because of their color, how they look, or how they smell. Choose flowers that will make you happy, because those will be the most effective for creating good feng shui in your home! And good energy adds to your

Magic Money vibe and keeps it flowing in your direction with ease.

Of course, feng shui goes beyond fresh flowers. In fact, flowers are just the tip of the iceberg. You can explore other options to your heart's (and wallet's) content.

When I noticed a difference from fresh flowers on Fridays, I got the idea to do something every day of the week. When I'm writing my daily lists, I focus on one aspect each day. Here are some ideas you might enjoy using:

Magic Money Monday

Every Monday I review my monthly goals and set an income goal for the week. Then, I break down income I'd like to receive that week into a daily goal. I promise you I almost never know where the money is going to come from, although a fair portion of my income is predictable (I get paid by certain clients at certain times of the month, and a few of my bonus checks and distributions arrive around the same time).

The key to success is to *have fun* with your Magic Money goal-setting. The fun is in deciding what number you'd love to see and then writing it down.

I can't tell you the number of times I've written down a number, crossed it out and doubled it—only to received that exact amount. About ten years ago, I wrote down $100,000 *for the week*, and I got it!

Keep in mind I'm a pragmatic person, but I had decided on a vehicle I wanted to buy. I also hate finance charges. I figured if I could manifest the money, that would be a clear sign I could buy the car. When FedEx knocked on my door with a signed contract and a check for the entire amount (I had requested six monthly installments), I just smiled and headed to the bank!

You may have to work up to the bigger numbers, which I'm sure goes without saying. I started working with my Magic Money Philosophy over twenty-five years ago. It didn't happen overnight for me, and if it takes even a year or two for you to feel like you've truly got the hang of it, there's nothing wrong with that!

If I hadn't manifested the money I needed to buy the car all at one time, I would have determined a percentage of each bit of income to put into a special savings account. Just as you have a savings account you are regularly putting money into; you can easily open a separate account and use it to save for something specific.

Of course, you do have the option to leap frog over any limiting beliefs you have about money and manifesting and step right into the equivalent of my year twenty manifesting abilities. This idea is one of the reasons I wrote these books, and I would be first in line to cheer you on and be thrilled for you.

Intention Tuesday!

On Tuesdays mornings, like every morning, I write my daily list. Then I review my Master Manifestation List and set an intention for the rest of the week.

My intention for this week is to receive an additional $25,000, which I will need to manifest because I'm on vacation (yes, I write, even on vacation). I also intend to finish a project I've been working on for the past six months when I return from vacation. Finally, I want to commence another one. Of course, I have no idea how I'll manifest the cash, but I do know I control my actions and my intentions.

The first step to receiving, getting, or achieving is clarity, and that's what Intention Tuesday is all about: gaining clarity about what I want. On Tuesdays, you can set an intention for the week and make it something amazing! Something you have no idea how it could come to pass or something so incredible you will know your manifesting muscles are getting bigger and stronger.

Then, give thanks you will receive your intention, at the perfect time, in the perfect way. Then, get on with your day.

What's Up, Wednesday?

Wednesday mornings I take a moment to look back over the last week and see how far I've come—how is my progress for this week? This month? Things are always looking up, and Wednesdays are a great day to notice the trends.

Wednesdays are a great time to review past intentions and see what you've manifested and make note. Say a silent prayer of gratitude for the things that have shown up and also for what hasn't shown up quite yet.

Thankful Thursday

Gratitude turns me into a money magnet, and it will do the same for you. Are you noticing what great things are happening all around you (or are you getting stuck on things that don't make you feel so great)? The part of your first Magic Money 30-Day Experiment where you kept a running list **of what** is a great habit to continue. If I haven't had time to add to my list over the past week, Thursdays are the days I "catch up" and make a note of everything.

Self-Care Saturday

I always wake up full of excitement for the plans I've made for the weekend, and it always involves some self-care practice (manicure, pedicure, massage, facial, etc.). Then, I let the magic take over and see what happens next.

Sometimes I review my week to see what I put on my list that has manifested, other times I just live in the moment. Magic money loves fun, remember? And, magic money is about your being-ness, not necessarily your doing-ness (except for those tried-and-true magic money practices from *Advanced Magic Money*). Focus on having fun, enjoying your time alone, or with friends, clients, and family.

Sunday Funday

I know, more fun! Of course!

When I was growing up, everything was closed on Sundays. You went to church (if your family was into that sort of thing), you came home and had lunch, and then you rested. While my life is a little different now (I attend my old church by tuning in online), I still love to rest on Sundays, and most importantly, do something fun.

If you're still working on living the life of your dreams and putting in time at a job while you create your dream career, take at least a few hours on Sunday for some fun. You could do your version of an Artist's Date from Julia Cameron's *The Artist's Way*, see a matinee, or even take a nice, long delicious nap. You could go on a date with your spouse (or one of your kids), go shopping with the money in your fun account, or indulge in Netflix binge (remember to make some popcorn)!

Your subconscious mind steers your destiny, and engaging in fun on a regular basis is a terrific subconscious mind activator. The more your mind associates "fun" with "money," the more and faster it will come into your life!

Engaging in a Magic Money practice some or most days of the week will help you become a Magic Money Master in the easiest and fastest way. But, of course, I have a few more tricks up my sleeve, in case you want 'em. Smile.

Chapter Six

PROSPERITY PRACTICES FOR MORE MAGIC MONEY

By the time you get to this part of the Magic Money Philosophy, you may be like me: addicted. I love the idea I can tap into unlimited abundance without stress, hard work, or compromising my integrity.

Magic Money eventually becomes a "do it and let it" type of lifestyle. Getting and staying in the flow of magic money requires just a bit of action on your part, and combined with thoughts and words that keep it coming in, you will enjoy this lifetime of abundance I've been sharing with you.

Consistency + Fun = Magic Money Mastery

As you know, I haven't always been as consistent with my thoughts, words, and actions as I am today. I've learned my lessons the hard way—by living in abundance, getting comfortable, and then starting over because I got out of those habits. When the going got tough, I would remember I had these practices *that work like a charm* and started again.

My intention for you is you read these books, engage in the magic money, and never quit! But there is a silver lining to my era of trial and error.

In my thirty-year study and development of the Magic Money Philosophy, I have discovered many ways to keep the magic and money flowing into my life. You don't have to do the same things over and over; there are lots of different tactics for keeping the money flowing and the miracles coming your way.

I'm going to share a half-dozen or so of my favorites. When you discover one I haven't mentioned, be sure to hop into the Magic Money Books Facebook Group and share your favorite!

Tip Like a Billionaire.

Fifteen percent is a typical gratuity when dining out or getting spa services. Your standard tip adds just $30 to a $200 dinner. The next time you receive terrific service, leave a terrific tip! Imagine tipping $50 instead, or twenty-five percent. While you're at it, think about the amount you're adding to your server. You can even mention the fact that their excellent service inspired your increased tip.

Not everyone can afford to tip well, but a practitioner of the Magic Money Philosophy (you!) can afford a few extra dollars.

Even as you're figuring out the tip and writing it on the check, say to yourself, *As money goes out, it immediately comes back to me multiplied!*

I'm not surprised anymore when I look at my email and I've sold something, or I receive an email notification of a new client just after I've tipped generously. It took a few dozen times for me to realize my affirmation had, indeed, come to pass and *as money goes out, it immediately returns to me multiplied!* And by immediately, folks, I do mean almost as quickly or even simultaneous to my giving!

No Mess, No Stress.

You might have heard cleanliness is next to Godliness, and whoever said it was spot on. I believe keeping my environments in order has contributed significantly to my financial freedom. I know cleanliness begets wealthiness.

Isn't it a cool idea to entertain you can bring more money into your life by taking a few minutes to clean up and get organized?

I'm not a clean freak, yet I have noticed I function better in a clean environment. A clean house isn't just "nice to have," it's considered a necessity for good mental and physical health. There is a correlation between clean houses and healthy people, and I know there's also a connection between clean spaces and wealthy people.

Catherine Ponder talks about the concept of divine order. I read about it in her book *The Dynamic Laws of Prosperity* so many years ago and found as I got everything organized I would prosper unexpectedly. And wouldn't you know, every time I would begin again after getting off track, I would start with cleaning out my closets, drawers, and even my car. And every time, I would experience a windfall, receive some unexpected income, or even get a dividend I wasn't expecting.

If you're in the place of feeling a little more financial tightness than you'd like, stop what you're doing and spend an hour cleaning up a messy space.

Although she doesn't stress money as an underlying reason for getting one's life in order, Marie Kondo hits on the happiness a clean environment brings in *The Life-Changing Magic of Tidying Up*.

Unless you're a real hoarder, you can get things cleaned up in short order. I tend to live a minimalist lifestyle, but clutter can still sneak up on me (especially with the other members of my family, not that I'm throwing anyone under the bus). Take one space at a time, such as a closet or bedside table drawer and get rid of anything you don't need. It will be an interesting experiment, and one you'll get a kick out of watching work in your favor.

PROSPERITY PRACTICES FOR MORE MAGIC

As You Pray, Move Your Feet.

When you feel lack or limitation, add an affirmation your self-talk while simultaneously cleaning out a messy space. If you receive an unexpected invoice or bill, or you are spending money faster than it is coming in, repeat something positive (*I am a money magnet! I receive money all the time! I have so much money!*) while you get that kitchen junk drawer or your pantry in order.

Feeling stressed about money? Take your car to the car wash or hire a detail specialist and get it "new car clean." The Universe is in charge of your bank account; you are in control of how dusty your bookcase is and how clean those Italian countertops can be! While you're waiting for another magic money infusion, make sure you don't have any you don't need, want, or love—and everything you do have is fabulous (just like you)!

Tackle Your Bedroom Closet.

Keep only clothes in your current size. If you gain weight, you'll want new clothes. If you lose weight, you'll want new clothes! I also do a load of wash every couple of days, so I tend not to have an overflowing laundry basket.

Get rid of any clothing that needs repair, is worn out, out of style, or goes unworn for extended periods of time.

Then, the Rest of the House.

Oprah is famous for saying, *Your home should rise to meet you.* I love walking into a clean home, whether it's after a long vacation, work trip, or a run to the supermarket. If you can afford to have a daily housekeeper (yup, just like if you lived in a hotel), go for it!

If not, make a daily cleaning list and keep everything in order by tackling it one day at a time. I don't have the time or inclination to clean my entire home over several hours. Instead, I do a little each day. One day, I dust. Another, I vacuum. Another day, I sweep and mop my floors, and on yet another day, I wipe down my countertops. I don't have hours to clean, and neither do you (and even having a weekly housekeeper doesn't keep a house clean for long).

By doing something for ten to fifteen minutes every day you'll keep your environment in order, and that magic money flowing in!

Be sure to calendar bigger cleaning jobs a few times a year, such as cleaning out your refrigerator, and having your carpets shampooed (because we have animals, I have ours cleaned every month or two), and cleaning windows and base boards.

Let the Work Money Flow!

Keep your desk clutter free, and give it a wipe down every week or so to keep dust bunnies from multiplying. Are the files on your computer a hot mess? Do you have 7,394 unread emails and an inbox that would make a reasonable person faint? Money doesn't like a cluttered environment, no matter what the situation! If there's any part of your work life that needs a good cleaning, schedule time to get them organized. Your bank accounts will soon be overflowing with new abundance.

Touch Everything Once

One way to stay clutter-free and become a magnet for money is to touch everything just once. Money likes efficiency, and the more efficient you are, the more money will come to you. Let me share just a few examples: LIST

Mail.

When I grab the mail, I open it by the trash can and throw away everything I don't need (flyers, mailers, solicitations, advertisements). I keep only the items that need action. Magazines that allow digital-only subscriptions are my new favorite, and those end up on my iPad. Those I still get, I read and recycle. If there's something I want to keep, I scan it into Evernote.

Packages and packaging.

Do you have an Amazon habit like me? Of course you do. (Smile.) A strong Amazon habit means you receive padded envelopes, boxes, and packing paper on a regular (daily?) basis. The community I live in has a recycling center, so I keep a stack of packing materials in my laundry room and make a weekly recycling run (and I always keep a set to reuse whenever possible).

Receipts, bills, leases, legal documents, and invoices.

Our lives are full of paper, and I do not love paper. Unless I will need to produce a hard copy (ever), I scan the original onto my hard drive (and to Evernote) and then shred it. If I might need it later, I keep it in my tiny filing cabinet and eventually move it to storage until I no longer need it.

Speaking of Evernote

I love this app! S. J. Scott has a great book, Master Evernote, and it is a terrific resource. After my initial read, I spent about three hours reviewing it and putting its suggestions in place. Now, I can put my fingers on just about any document, resource, or even recipe I need. By keeping digital copies of everything, I'm ready for just about anything.

A Clean, Well-Maintained Car is... Awesome.

I know I just mentioned getting your car cleaned, and it's worth a second, significant mention. Cars are expensive, and most of us spend a considerable amount of time in them. Just like your home and work environments, keeping your vehicles clean keeps abundance flowing. My cars get regular weekly washes and quarterly detailing. Immediately after a long trip, they get some extra tender loving care right away.

In what feels like another lifetime, I have had an unexpected passenger. There is almost nothing as embarrassing as apologizing to someone for the mess. Once I decided I wanted my car to be clean in case I was riding in it, I not only no longer had to apologize, I enjoyed lots of compliments! *Wow, what a clean car!* Even the occasional, *Man, your car smells great!*

A final note on cleanliness—Keeping clean homes, offices, and vehicles isn't only about abundance or other people. You will love having stress-free spaces in which to spend your time, create magic moments, and recharge your batteries. Your spaces should be kept in order because *you* are there, and you deserve to feel in divine order as much of the time as possible.

Trigger Devices are the Bomb-Diggity!

What gets our attention grows and expands, sometimes quick like a bunny! In our busy lives, it helps to have easy reminders to keep focused and on track because there is nothing like manifesting something fast only to realize it is the opposite of what we wanted. Just like having an everyday practice, identifying items to use as trigger devices helps you to stay focused on magic money practices. A trigger device is simply an item that reminds you to do, say, or think something specific. So, even when an unexpected project demands your attention, you have a sick kid, or the toilet overflows and takes up an unexpected hour of your time, you'll have ways to remember to keep magic money on its way to you!

First, identify something you want to do, think, or say on a regular basis. Second, identify an item (such as a penny, a keychain or even a coffee mug) that can trigger you to think, say, or do it. Finally, assign an action, intention, or even affirmation to your trigger device.

My trigger devices remind me to:

- Mentally review my current goals and visualize them as already achieved.
- Give thanks for a few things in my life. Because gratitude is a magic money accelerant, remember?
- Say an affirmation.
- Do whatever I've attached to that item, sound, or situation.

You can also identify something that isn't physical as a reminder, such as an alarm on your phone, a certain song, or even a commercial on television.

Here are a few of my favorite trigger devices and their function for me:

- **A Penny for Your Thoughts.** I carry a new (current year) penny in my pocket every day. I put it in my pocket when I get dressed in the morning, and leave it on the counter at night when I go to bed. Every time I put my hands in my pockets throughout the day, I notice the penny. It reminds me to focus on something I'm grateful for that day.

- **Phone Alarms.** I have reminder alarms on my phone for lots of different things, and among them is an alarm to take a moment to express some gratitude. The alarm, simply labeled "gratitude," reminds me to take a minute and super-charge my vibration with a shot of gratitude.

- **A Keychain.** When I set my sights on a new car, I roll down the dealership to take it for a test drive. Before I leave, I get some merchandise to keep me focused on my new target. Every time I leave home, I see the keychain I'm going to put my new car keys on, and it reminds me of my intention. I say a silent "Thanks in advance, Universe!" before I go on my way. To date, I've driven every single dream car I've ever wanted (except the one I'm mentally affirming right now).

- **A Visit to the Restroom.** Yes, I'm serious. Every time I go to the bathroom, I say a specific affirmation as I wash my hands. If I'm alone, I say it out loud. If I'm in a public place, I say it silently to myself.

The possibilities with this practice are endless. Trigger devices are useful because they help us effortlessly stay on the magic money track. A few minutes of preparation can lead to lots of magic money flowing your way!

You could get a special keychain, use an alarm, or even put a sign up on the inside of your front door. You could even use a common car as a trigger device. Every time you see a Tesla, it could remind you of a trip you want to take to Hawaii. You spend a minute visualizing sipping a piña colada beachside on Maui, thank the Universe, and get on with the rest of your day. It's up to you, just have fun with this idea because it is a fun idea to work with.

Find a Penny, Pick it Up ... and ...

As I've mentioned, I find money somewhere every single day. In in the lobby of our vacation hotel, I found three shiny new pennies under the chair when we had dinner. Finding money reminds me there is an abundance all around me. It focuses my mind on this fact, and I say a quick thank you for this truth.

When you find money, let it be a reminder to you. Allow those quarters, dimes, nickels and pennies to trigger you in a most positive way.

The Time has Come

You're in the final stretch, and as you read these last two chapters, I hope you are as excited as I am for what's to come. There are a couple of ideas I want to cover before I turn you loose to live your life of magic and miracles.

Chapter Seven

MAGIC EVERYTHING

What You Want Can Come to You in Magical Ways, at the Perfect Time, in an Easy Way

Now you know: any intention you set can manifest in any number of ways. In fact, although these books seemingly are just about "magic money" they could be retitled to "magic everything."

The truth is this: your desired good can and will come to you through literally millions of channels. It can come in the form of money to buy what you want; you can receive it as a gift, you could even find it in your mailbox. Just as there are multiple ways money can come to you, *not just through your job or one person*, so can everything on your list.

You've heard the saying (and we've briefly discussed), *Timing is everything.* Holy smokes—this's the mother of all accurate statements! You'll want to wrap your brain around the idea there is the perfect time for everything as soon as possible.

It is very easy to say, *I want $10,000 today*, and be disappointed when it doesn't show up. You might not get $10,000 today, because the Universe wants to give you $11,500 tomorrow and is working out the details.

Expanding from magic money is something you *do*, to magic money is who you *are* is a process. My goal was to transition full-time into a magic money mindset, and that is my goal for you.

It took me awhile to loosen my grip and finally let the Universe take the wheel. I had to adopt a mindset, the intricacies of which I'm about to share with you. What I didn't realize was the tighter I held on to a specific desire, and the more I tried to control the outcome (any outcome!), the more I stood in the way of the result I desired.

The stress I experienced wasn't worth it or even necessary—and eventually, I realized I could "let go and let God" and the situation would work out, for the highest good of all concerned.

Imagine that!

There is a time for everything. Although we can influence our magic money timing, we don't truly have the final say. It is easy to stay positive when we are experiencing the flow of magic money. A challenge you might enounter is staying positive when you see little, if any, magic money.

Enter ...

A Lifetime of Magic Money Mindset

The person with a Magic Money Mindset remains focused on the positive and unmoved from their positive mindset *no matter what evidence appears to the contrary*. You look disaster right in the whites of their eyes and see only what you want to see. While others are losing their minds, careening into a downward spiral of negative emotions and self-talk, you focus your positive thoughts, words, and actions solely on the outcome you desire.

Easier said than done, you say. Well, after some practice, you'll find it easier to kick back, relax, and wait for the positive outcome you desired all along.

Think, Say, Do, and Know: All is Well

The work you have done up to this point has prepared you for the level of inner and outer calm you must maintain, even as things seem to spiral out of control. You have built the magic money muscles you'll need as you face challenges, big and small, monetary, physical, emotional, or spiritual.

No matter what, trust me when I say, *All is well.*

But I'm sure you're thinking, *Okay, Holly, but how do I maintain this zen-like magic money state?*

I'm so glad you asked.

Think

It is easy to think ourselves into several shades of crazy when we're faced with an unpleasant or downright awful situation. But, my magic money friend, your thoughts are incredibly powerful, and it is critical you grab 'em and reign 'em in the moment you realize they are not serving you.

When the proverbial shiznit hits the fan, I've trained myself to wonder what good is at work in this situation. I'm not always able to do it in the first fifteen minutes, but I've gotten good at it and so will you.

To say I've weathered some storms is a wild understatement, and it only took about three thousand of them (give or take) before I got the message: out of every disaster comes something delightful.

We have and will face obstacles and challenges; there's no doubt about it. But you can maintain your sanity and positive attitude, especially if you decide in advance how you're going to handle them. I even submit you greatly influence their outcome by adopting these practices.

Need extra money for a car repair? There's always more than enough when you need it.

Facing a life-threatening illness? Laughter is the best medicine, combined with positive thoughts and words.

Going through a tough divorce? It will be over before you know it, and you'll be happily building your new, amazing life.

Get an unexpected bill in the mail? Congratulations, someone trusted you with goods or services and allowed you to pay later. Now you can manifest it like the star you are!

All is well no matter what, I promise, all is well.

After you learn about your new situation, just take a moment, and think to yourself, *Hmmm. I wonder what the good is in this situation?* (Remember your PPQs from *Advanced Magic Money.*) The good might be that you have yet another chance to prove to yourself the Universe has your back, or you're manifesting heavyweight champion of the world today.

Remain calm, and think to yourself: *the Universe has got this!* And isn't it going to be fun to sit back, unattached, and see how?

Yes, yes, it is! But wait, there's more!

Say and Do

Next, you're going to say something, and then you're going to do something. I mean, it's only natural to talk about what is happening. But now, you're armed with tools that can accelerate great results, and even possibly reverse "bad" ones.

Remember your first Magic Money Experiment in *Beginning Magic Money*? No complaining, bemoaning, or bellyaching. Now that you know not to do them, you can't just go back to the way you were! If anything, you must double down and refuse to say anything you don't want to manifest and become your reality.

My first inclination used to be to "process the situation" (otherwise known as *complain out loud to multiple people*). Then I would try to control the situation by doing whatever I could think of to do.

Now, I might run the situation by someone to see if there's something I'm missing. But not until after I've gotten quiet, blessed the situation as good, and said an affirmation (or fifty). And, I limit my conversations to quick check-ins, not elaborate story-telling therapy sessions. Then, I wait. I get busy either doing something productive (blessing, reading, cleaning, organizing, or working on a project) or I get busy doing nothing.

You'll want to use some of the same Magic Money Affirmations I say that can handle just about every difficult situation.

"*All is well*" is one of those affirmations. The affirmation that doubles as a blessing: "*I bless this situation as good, good, good!*" is another.

Before you go down the rabbit hole, making the situation even more emotional than it is, take a deep breath, and a moment to say, *All is well. I bless this situation as good, good, good!* Say it out loud as many times as you need to, and if it helps, clean something while you're at it. (I can't be the only one who feels less stressed in a clean environment, right?)

When I'm experiencing a challenge, I say a poem I first heard about twenty-five years ago. If necessary, I say it, write it, and think it over and over until I feel a sense of peace. Here it is:

I believe I am always divinely guided.

I believe I always take the right turn in the road.

I believe God always makes a way where there is no way.

You can always change "God" to "the Universe" or whatever works for you. The point is the words, combined with your intentional, positive action will provide comfort and release your intention simultaneously.

When something, *anything*, is going wrong, you must control what you can control! Say out loud exactly what you want to happen. With conviction. Until you believe it. For example:

- I will find the lost key! (I mean, I never lose anything!)
- I will get/receive the money I need in the nick of time (with plenty to share and spare)!
- I'm going to crush it and finish that project on time!
- There will be a quick and peaceful, healthy, or positive resolution to this situation!
- I know everything is working out for everyone's highest good. I bless this situation and everyone on it.

You cannot, even for a moment, entertain the worst thing your imagination can come up with is what will happen. The moment you realize you started the sentence, *I hope he doesn't ...* Cancel that out and replace it with, *I know he's is going to ... {insert something positive here}.*

These practices will lead to your *knowing*.

Know

Everything is always working out for your highest good. And, from now on, you're going to *think, say, do,* and *know* so.

Your mind is all powerful. What you focus on expands, and you can adopt a knowingness to carry you through those tough situations.

But I'm Stressed, Holly!

Have you heard nothing I've said? Just kidding! I'm not saying anything here I haven't experienced myself. I mean, how many times did I have to start over? Of course, this is why I'm covering this topic again, one last time, before I end this series.

The more you stress, cogitate on your situation, and try to work it out in your mind, the longer you suffer unnecessarily. Am I talking only about money? Nope. But let's stay focused on the topic at hand for a moment. The more you stress about "where the money is coming from," the longer it is going to take. Fear is a money repellent because it is the strongest of negative vibrations, and it acts to repel abundance.

If you're truly stressed about a situation, and I'm sure there will be times when you are, the only thing you can control is "the controllables." Yup, you guessed it: the controllables are what you think, say, do, and know.

Gratitude is the opposite vibration: it stabilizes the situation (and you!) and magnetizes your good to you in record time. A true magic money mindset is based on, and centered, and solidified, in gratitude. Do everything you can, in good times and bad, to be grateful.

Even as you are amid a mess, identify what you want. Then, keep your eyes open for it, be thankful for everything you already have, and be ready to receive it when the time is right.

Remember: Be-ing not Do-ing

I'm going to switch gears just a little and say I get a huge kick out of watching people spin themselves into a tizzy trying to *do* everything "right."

Authors share multiple covers, looking for approval and to others to help them choose which one is the best. Internet marketers do "A/B" testing to see what gets more clicks or likes or shares. People place multiple ads with different copy to see which one performs the best. I'm a fan of math and data, but ultimately, I know what is much more powerful is the energy and vibration emanating from the person.

We've all seen amateur movies that have gone viral, individuals who are not exactly cover models but have that "certain something" who have been blessed with unexplainable success and read books panned by critics that become worldwide bestsellers.

I believe in every situation, each of these was blessed because of the intention of the person who created the project and who they were being.

So, Who are YOU Being?

You are a magical being with the unlimited power to bring absolutely anything you desire into your life.

And, your only assignment is to come to the party with your party hat on, positively expectant you'll find what and who you want to find, ready to dance.

Even if you have white man's overbite and your dance style is less than ideal (or is that just me?), it's still your job to be ready to dance at any moment.

When you're all suited up, it's time to begin Your Final Magic Money Experiment. I'm ready when you are!

Chapter Eight

A LIFETIME OF MAGIC MONEY:
Your Final Magic Money Experiment

Wooooo hooooooo! You made it—you've read all three of the books that make up the Magic Money Course in Creating Abundance.

You've discovered there's always more than enough of everything you need (including money, duh!), and probably that the Universe has a wicked fun sense of humor.

You have some walkin' around money (as my grandmother used to say), given away money to make the world a better place, saved some money for crazy good opportunities to come or even future generations, and had some amazing fun along the way.

You might be expecting that Your Final Magic Money Experiment is something crazy amazingly great. And you'd be right.

Here it is:

Continue to do everything you've learned until your Magic Money Intention is how you live every day.

The Magic Money Philosophy will no longer be a list of things you do; they become who you are—daily habits you do automatically, thoughts and words you speak without thinking.

Remember my Magic Money Intention?

I always have more than enough to give, save, share, and spare, and my needs and desires are always met (on time or early).

I only wrote these books because others around me found my powers of manifestation awe-inspiring. To me, normal. No thought required.

I receive money; I allocate it.

I face a challenge, I bless it, say a few other affirmations about it, and get on with my day.

I see a new pair of shoes I want? I say, *Wouldn't it be nice if a pair of those babies showed up in my closet?* Then, I get an email saying they are 50% off or I find myself in a store where they are on clearance—or my husband's best friend's mom says, "Holly, I think we're the same shoe size. Would you have any interest in these shoes I bought and never wore?"

Yes, all of those and so much more. Automatic, just like my coffee maker.

Your Final Magic Money Experiment is to live the Magic Money Philosophy for the rest of your life. Keep starting over until you get it and it gets you. Play with it, have *fun* with it. Share it! Wouldn't it be wonderful if everyone you knew was manifesting more of everything they've always wanted?

That is why I wrote these books and shared the Magic Money Philosophy with you because

A LIFETIME OF MAGIC MONEY

I want you to live a life of magic money and miracles and everything you heart desires.

Here's to your lifetime of Magic Money!

GRATITUDE

A huge bucket of thanks to my Experimenters and Magic Money Practitioners!

Thank you for validating my process. Wishing you a lifetime of magic money and abundance of every wonderful thing!

WHO IS HOLLY

Holly Alexander is the author of the three-book series: *Magic Money:* A Course in Creating Abundance. She's a serial entrepreneur, multiple-business owner, philanthropist, wife, mom, avid traveler, reader, and explorer.

She believes you can have, do, and be everything you want to have, do, and be when you treat life and money with the respect they deserve. You can find out more at MagicMoneyBooks.com.

Notes

NOTES

Notes

Notes

Notes

Notes

Notes

Notes

Notes

Notes

Made in the USA
San Bernardino, CA
10 October 2018